ENIGMAS *of* HISTORY

THE LEGEND OF KING ARTHUR

WORLD BOOK

a Scott Fetzer company
Chicago
www.worldbook.com

World Book edition of "Enigmas de la historia" by Editorial Sol 90.

Enigmas de la historia
La leyenda del Rey Arturo

This edition licensed from Editorial Sol 90 S.L.

Enigmas of History
The Legend of King Arthur

World Book, Inc.
233 North Michigan Avenue
Suite 2000
Chicago, Illinois, 60601 U.S.A.

For information about other World Book publications, visit our website at **www.worldbook.com** or call **1-800-967-5325.**

Library of Congress Cataloging-in-Publication Data

Leyenda del Rey Arturo. English
The legend of King Arthur. -- English-language edition.
pages cm. -- (Enigmas of history)
Originally published as: La leyenda del Rey Arturo, by Editorial Sol S.L., c2013.
Includes index.
Summary: "An exploration of the questions and mysteries that have puzzled scholars and experts about the legends of King Arthur, the Roundtable, and his knights. Features include a map, fact boxes, biographies of famous experts on Arthurian legend, places to see and visit, a glossary, further readings, and index"--Provided by publisher.
ISBN 978-0-7166-2664-0
1. Arthur, King--Juvenile literature. 2. Britons--Kings and rulers--Juvenile literature. 3. Great Britain--History--To 1066--Juvenile literature. 4. Great Britain--Antiquities, Celtic--Juvenile literature. 5. Arthurian romances--Juvenile literature. I. World Book, Inc. II. Title.
DA152.5.A7L4913 2014
942.01'4--dc23

2014006446

Set ISBN: 978-0-7166-2660-2

Printed in China by PrintWORKS Global Services, Shenzhen, Guangdong
1st printing May 2014

King Arthur, the legendary ruler of medieval Britain, is depicted in a fragment of a tapestry made in the Low Countries in the early 1400's. A real English leader named Arthur probably existed, but historians know little about him. Storytellers may have based tales about King Arthur on this actual leader who won minor victories over German invaders in the early A.D. 500's.

Tapestry Fragment With King Arthur (c. 1400) wool warp and wool wefts, The Metropolitan Museum of Art (Universal History Archive/UIG/Bridgeman Art Library)

Staff

Executive Committee

President
Donald D. Keller

Vice President and Editor in Chief
Paul A. Kobasa

Vice President, Sales
Sean Lockwood

Vice President, Finance
Anthony Doyle

Director, Marketing
Nicholas A. Fryer

Director, Human Resources
Bev Ecker

Editorial

Associate Director, Annuals and Topical Reference
Scott Thomas

Managing Editor, Annuals and Topical Reference
Barbara A. Mayes

Senior Editor, Annuals and Topical Reference
Christine Sullivan

Manager, Indexing Services
David Pofelski

Administrative Assistant
Ethel Matthews

Manager, Contracts & Compliance (Rights & Permissions)
Loranne K. Shields

Editorial Administration Director, Systems and Projects
Tony Tills

Senior Manager, Publishing Operations
Timothy Falk

Manufacturing/Production

Director
Carma Fazio

Manufacturing Manager
Barbara Podczerwinski

Production/Technology Manager
Anne Fritzinger

Proofreader
Nathalie Strassheim

Graphics and Design

Art Director
Tom Evans

Senior Designer
Don Di Sante

Media Researcher
Jeff Heimsath

Manager, Cartographic Services
Wayne K. Pichler

Senior Cartographer
John M. Rejba

Marketing

Marketing Manager
Tamika Robinson

Marketing Specialist
Annie Suhy

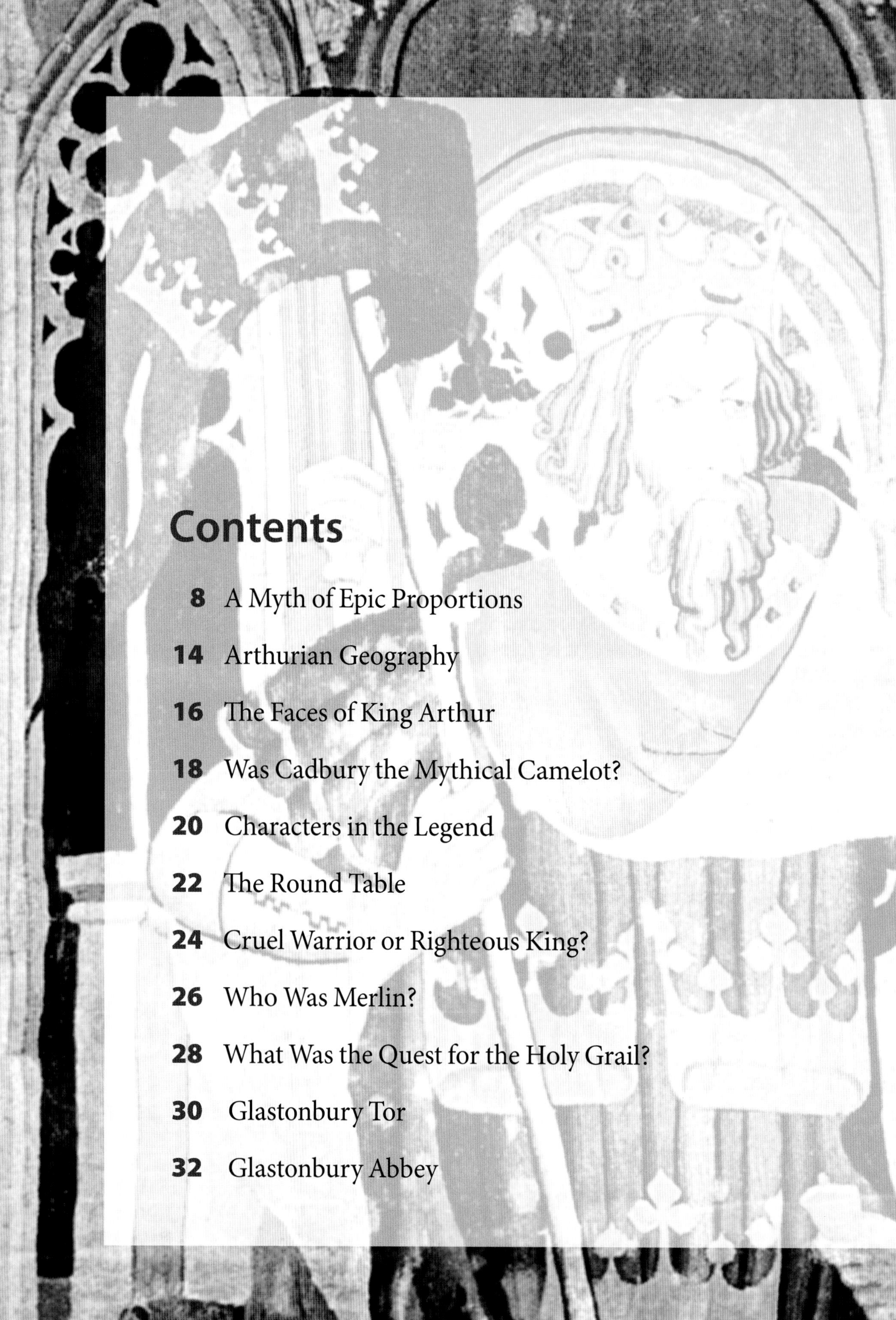

Contents

TINTAGEL CHAPEL
in Cornwall, in southwestern England, is a popular destination for tourists seeking sites linked to King Arthur. According to legend, Arthur was born in the fortress of Tintagel. The small chapel there was built between 1080 and 1150, centuries after Arthur supposedly lived.

A Myth of Epic Proportions

Few legends have had as much power to fascinate people over time as that of King Arthur—despite a lack of historical evidence about this Celtic monarch.

The legend of King Arthur is one of Europe's greatest cultural myths. For more than 800 years, writers and poets—and now producers of television programs, movies, and even video games—have recounted Arthur's brave deeds and those of his Knights of the Round Table.

The legend of this mighty but doomed king grew from songs and tales about a tribal chief or military leader of the British Celts in the A.D. 500's. Like the Celts of continental Europe, the British Celts were mainly warriors and farmers. A priestly class called the Druids performed religious rituals and served as advisers to the tribal chiefs.

Over the centuries, Arthur's fame grew until he became a national hero. He even became the model for the sensible, brave, and just king.

CELTS UNDER ATTACK

In 55 B.C., the great Roman general Julius Caesar sailed across the English Channel from Gaul (now France) with a small force to explore what is now England. He returned the next year with an invading army and defeated some of the native Celtic tribes before returning to Rome. By the A.D. 90's, the Romans had conquered the southern part of the island of Britain, including present-day England and Wales. Although many Celts suffered under Roman rule, the Romans brought order to Britain, and England prospered.

After Roman forces left England in the early 400's to help defend Rome against Germanic invaders, England was thrown into turmoil. With the Romans gone, the British Celts could not protect themselves against invasion by people from Scotland called Picts and people from Ireland called Scots.

The greatest danger, however, came from seafaring Germanic tribes, especially the Angles, Saxons, and Jutes. After first raiding the coast, these tribes began to establish permanent settlements. The Jutes were probably the first tribe to land. The Angles and Saxons who followed set up kingdoms throughout southern and eastern England.

The British Celts fought back. But eventually, they were pushed to the north and west, until they controlled only the mountain areas of what are now Wales and Cornwall in the United Kingdom. Still, according to historical tradition, the Britons held out for a number of years under the leadership of a tribal chief. That leader might have been the inspiration for the Legend of King Arthur.

THE LEGEND BEGINS

Arthur first appears in some of the oldest-known Welsh poems

ARTHUR IN BRONZE
A statue of Arthur wearing his armor stands in the Royal Chapel in Innsbruck, Austria. It was designed by Albrecht Dürer in the 1520's.

and songs. Among them is a collection of songs, dated to the mid-500's, about the Celtic warriors who fell in battle against the Saxons.

In the 800's, a Welsh monk named Nennius produced a history of Britain that said, "Arthur, together with the kings of Britain, fought against them [the Saxons] in those days, and he was their Dux Bellorum [war leader]." According to Nennius, Arthur won 12 battles against the Saxons, the last of which was the Battle of Mount Badon. This clash is said to have stopped the Saxons' advance against the Celts. Nennius's history propelled Arthur from a local champion into a national hero.

The first document that claims the existence of a historical person named Arthur is the *Annales Cambriae (The Annals of Wales)*, written in Latin around A.D. 970. The book covers 500 years of the history of the Welsh people. Arthur is mentioned twice in this work. In the first mention, he is the leader of the Britons who defeated the Saxons in the Battle of Mount Badon in about 519. The second mention sets the date of the Battle of Camlann as 540. It describes how Arthur fought against his son (or nephew) Mordred and how they were both killed.

THE GOOD KING

The first narrative of the life of King Arthur from birth to death came from the pen of Geoffrey of Monmouth, a Welsh historian. Geoffrey tells of Arthur in his monumental work, *Historia Regum Brittaniae* (*History of the Kings of Britain*), published in 1136. With this story, Geoffrey established the basis of the Arthurian legend as we know it today.

In his history, Geoffrey relates events from the time when the Britons first occupied the island until they were defeated by the Anglo-Saxons. He starts with Brutus, the great-grandson of Aeneas, the mythical Trojan hero and ancestor of the Roman people. According to legend, Brutus settled in what is now London with a band of companions and became the first king of Britain. In this way, the Celts could say that they descended from the Trojans. Then Geoffrey writes of the Roman conquest, the magician Merlin, and Uther Pendragon, Arthur's father.

Geoffrey goes on to relate the legendary birth of Arthur, his education outside of the court, his ascension to the throne, his marriage to Guenevere, and his conquest of Wales, England, Iceland, Norway,

AMPHITHEATER
Located in Caerleon, Wales, the amphitheater (above right) had a capacity for 6,000 spectators. Its remains are still well preserved today. Some people have suggested that this building of Roman origin may have been the inspiration for King Arthur's famous Round Table.

FAMILY IN COMBAT
King Arthur fights against Sir Mordred in the Battle of Camlann, where both died. Later traditions presented Mordred as an illegitimate son of Arthur, the result of his relationship with his sister Morgan le Fay.

and Brittany (northwestern France). Geoffrey even describes how Arthur was crowned emperor by the pope. Geoffrey also recounts how Arthur fought and defeated his nephew Mordred, who tried to usurp his power.

Geoffrey claimed that his history came from "a very old book written in the British language." He said he had merely translated the text into Latin.

But modern scholars note that Geoffrey appears to have relied on the many written poems and narratives that had already established the myth of "the good king." Geoffrey also probably relied on additional accounts passed down by word of mouth that have not survived to modern times. Scholars have praised Geoffrey for displaying great creativity in merging eras, traditions, and locations. One noted scholar has said that Geoffrey's great achievement was presenting as historical something that seems to have been "pure invention."

ARTHUR'S FAME

The almost instant success of the *History of the Kings of Britain* pushed the Celtic and Welsh origins of the Arthurian legend into the background. Geoffrey's new version even spread to the courts of France.

Other authors soon began writing about Arthur. In 1155, the poet Robert Wace "created" the Round Table in his work *Roman de Brut (The Story of Brutus).* The book tells how Arthur decided to seat his knights around a circular table to avoid quarrels over who should occupy the seats of honor. Since the knights were all "noble and equal," no knight could then boast of sitting higher than his peers.

In 1180, Chrétien de Troyes, a poet at the court of a French queen, linked Arthur to the search for the Holy Grail in *Perceval,* or *The Tale of the Grail.* In de Troyes's unfinished poem, the Holy Grail is the cup used by Jesus at the Last Supper.

Robert de Boron, a French poet who lived at the end of the 1100's and beginning of the 1200's, connected the mythical Island of Avalon—where Arthur is said to rest until his return to the world of the living—with Glastonbury—the location, according to tradition, of the first Christian church on English soil.

LITERARY MASTERPIECES

In 1485, William Caxton, a well-known English printer, published *Le Morte d'Arthur (The Death of Arthur)* by Sir Thomas Malory, who had supposedly died in 1470. The book relates the entire story of King Arthur of Britain and the careers of such Knights of the Round Table as Lancelot, Gareth, and Tristan. *Le Morte d'Arthur* provides the fullest version of the legends about Arthur and his court ever written in English.

The English poet Edmund Spenser used the character of Arthur to discuss the qualities required of a gentleman in his epic poem *The Faerie Queene* (1590-1609). Another masterpiece of English literature that focuses on Arthur is Lord Tennyson's *Idylls of the King*, a series of 12 narrative poems published between 1842 and 1885.

MODERN TALES

Modern books about Arthur include Mark Twain's time-traveling book, *A Connecticut Yankee in King Arthur's Court* (1889); T. H. White's classic four-volume *The Once and Future King* (1958); Mary Stewart's masterful *The Merlin Trilogy* (1970-1979); and Rosemary Sutcliff's exciting *Sword at Sunset* (1987).

The Mists of Avalon (1987) and *Merlin's Harp* (1995) tell the story of Camelot from a feminine point of view. Bernard Cornwell's *Warlord Chronicles* (1995-1997) is richly detailed. In *Firelord* (1980) and *Beloved Exile* (1984), Parke Godwin imagines Arthur and Guenevere in historically accurate settings. A. A. Attanasio incorporates fantastical elements in the legend of Arthur in *The Dragon and the Unicorn* (1994), *The Eagle and the Sword* (1997), *The Wolf and the Crown* (1998), and *The Serpent and the Grail* (1999).

Geoffrey of Monmouth

(1100?-1155?)

A Welsh historian who wrote the first narrative of the entire life of King Arthur in *History of the Kings of Britain* (about 1136). Geoffrey claimed to have based his work on a chronicle. But most of the tale is probably his own invention.

Sir Thomas Malory

(?-1471)

The author of *Le Morte d'Arthur (The Death of Arthur).* The book provides the fullest version of the legends about Arthur and his court ever written in English. Scholars disagree on the identity of the author of *Le Morte d'Arthur.* A knight of Warwickshire, who was imprisoned for a series of crimes, is usually identified as the author. Malory's book has influenced the work of many artists and writers.

Leslie Alcock

(1925 - 2006)

One of the most prominent British archaeologists who researched the Dark Ages (the period between the 400's and 1000's) in Great Britain. He is the author of *Arthur's Britain* (1971), a key book on the subject. During excavations in South Cadbury, in the late 1960's, he found the remains of a fortified village from the Iron Age at the site which people in the area have referred to as Camelot for centuries. The site may have been occupied for thousands of years. He also found that in the 400's and 500's, the village was fortified again, and other structures, which included a great banquet hall, were built on the surrounding plateau.

Richard W. Barber

(1941 -)

A British historian who is considered a global authority on medieval history and an expert on the Arthurian legend. He is the author of *The Holy Grail,* one of the most in-depth books on the subject.

Philip Rahtz

(1921 - 2011)

A British archaeologist who carried out several excavations in Somerset, particularly in the areas around Cadbury Castle, where it is assumed that King Arthur lived.

A. C. Lewis Brown

(1869 - 1946)

American scholar who specialized in the origins of the Arthurian legends. He received his doctorate from Harvard in 1900 with his thesis, *Iwain: A Study in the Origins of Arthurian Romance,* in which he pointed out close links between the Arthurian chronicle and Celtic folklore.

His primary work, published three years after his death, is *The Origin of the Grail Legend* (1943). Another of his academic works, *The Round Table Before Wace,* is still often cited by historians and students interested in the legend of King Arthur.

Geoffrey Ashe

(1923 -)

British historian who analyzed the Arthurian legend. His most famous book is *King Arthur's Avalon: The Story of Glastonbury* (1957). In Ashe's *The Discovery of King Arthur* (1985), the focus is on the prophecies of the magician Merlin, who saw the imminent coming of the heroic monarch as well as Arthur's relations with his sister, Morgan le Fay.

Arthurian Geography

During the time of King Arthur, the British Isles were inhabited by various Celtic peoples (Britons, Scots, Picts) who lived in tribal groups. Numerous sites on the islands have been identified with important places in the life of Arthur and his knights.

Invasions of the British Isles

From the A.D. 300's onward, Roman England was invaded by tribal groups from northern Europe called the Angles, Jutes, and Saxons, who devastated the coastal communities on the eastern part of the island. After Roman forces left Britain, the Anglo-Saxons swept through much of the southern part of the island. According to tradition, the British Celts stopped the invaders' advance in the early 500's at the Battle of Mount Badon. Later accounts credited Arthur with leading the victorious Celts.

1 IRELAND

The island was inhabited by various Gaelic Celts, most notably the Scots, who invaded Scotland at the beginning of the 400's.

2 WALES

When ancient Rome invaded Britain in A.D. 43, the country was divided between various Celtic tribes, including the Cornovii, Deceangli, Demetae, Ordovices, and Silures.

The Birthplace of Arthur

According to legend, Lady Igraine gave birth to Arthur in the fortress of Tintagel in Cornwall. At the base of the cliff, where ruins of the castle remain to this day, is "Merlin's cave." There, the wizard and Uther Pendragon supposedly conspired to seduce Igraine.

3 BRITANNIA

In 55 B.C., the great Roman general Julius Caesar sailed across the English Channel from Gaul (now France) with a small force to explore England. He returned the next year with an invading army and defeated some of the native tribes before returning to Rome. In A.D. 43, the Roman Emperor Claudius ordered Roman armies to invade Britannia, as the island was then called. The Romans easily conquered the native tribes in the southeast.

Cornwall

Many locations linked to King Arthur are in Cornwall, in southwestern England. Notable among these places is Tintagel, where the legend of King Arthur begins.

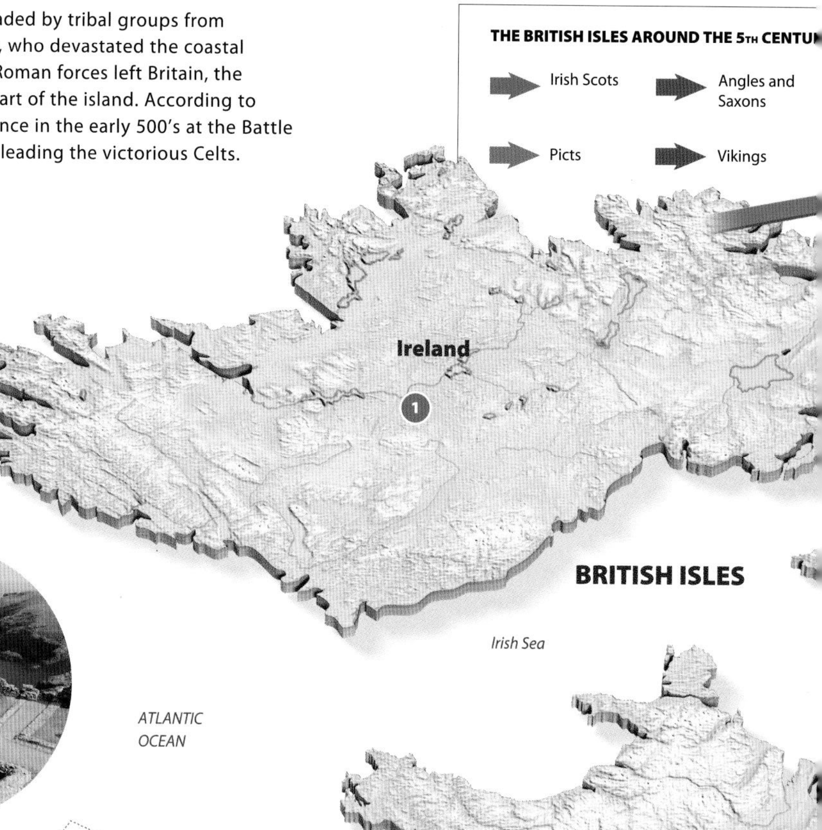

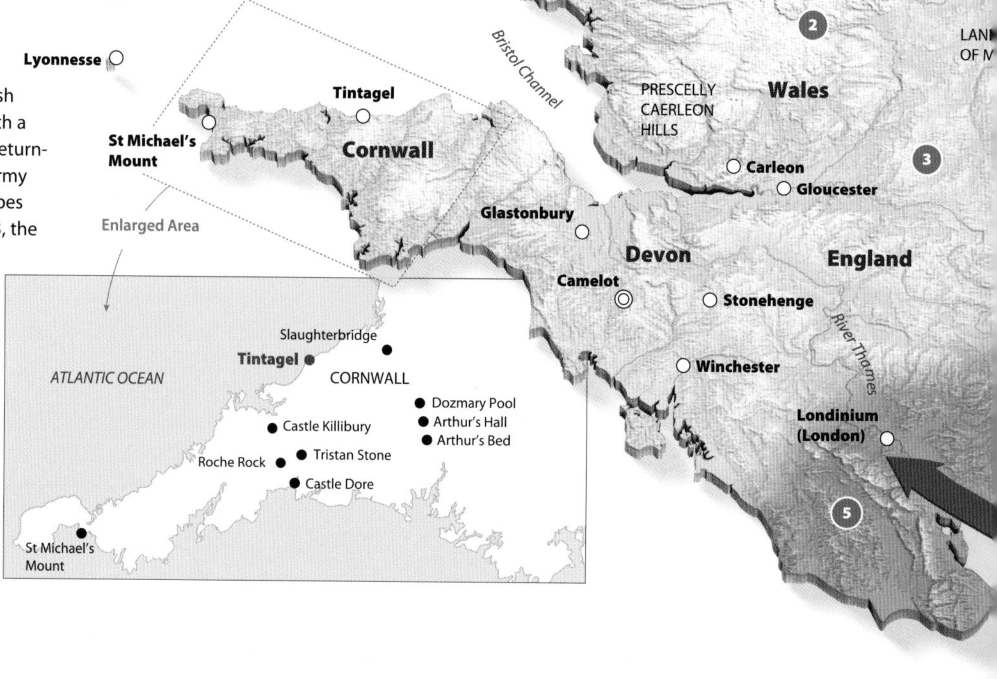

THE BRITISH ISLES AROUND THE 5TH CENTU

Irish Scots
Angles and Saxons
Picts
Vikings

Ireland
BRITISH ISLES
Irish Sea
ATLANTIC OCEAN
Bristol Channel
Lyonnesse
Tintagel
St Michael's Mount
Cornwall
Enlarged Area
PRESCELLY CAERLEON HILLS
Wales
Carleon
Gloucester
Glastonbury
Devon
Camelot
Stonehenge
England
River Thames
Winchester
Londinium (London)

ATLANTIC OCEAN
Slaughterbridge
Tintagel
CORNWALL
Dozmary Pool
Arthur's Hall
Arthur's Bed
Castle Killibury
Roche Rock
Tristan Stone
Castle Dore
St Michael's Mount

Is "Arthur's Stone" Connected with the Legendary British King?

A piece of slate discovered in 1998 at Tintagel Castle in Cornwall carries the Latin inscription "Pater Coliavificit Artognov," which has been translated as "Artognou, descendant of Paternus Colus, made this." The slate, which has been dated to the A.D. 500's, is informally known as "Arthur's Stone." "Artognou" was probably pronounced as "Arth-new." Archaeologists involved in the discovery, however, doubt that the stone is connected to the legendary king.

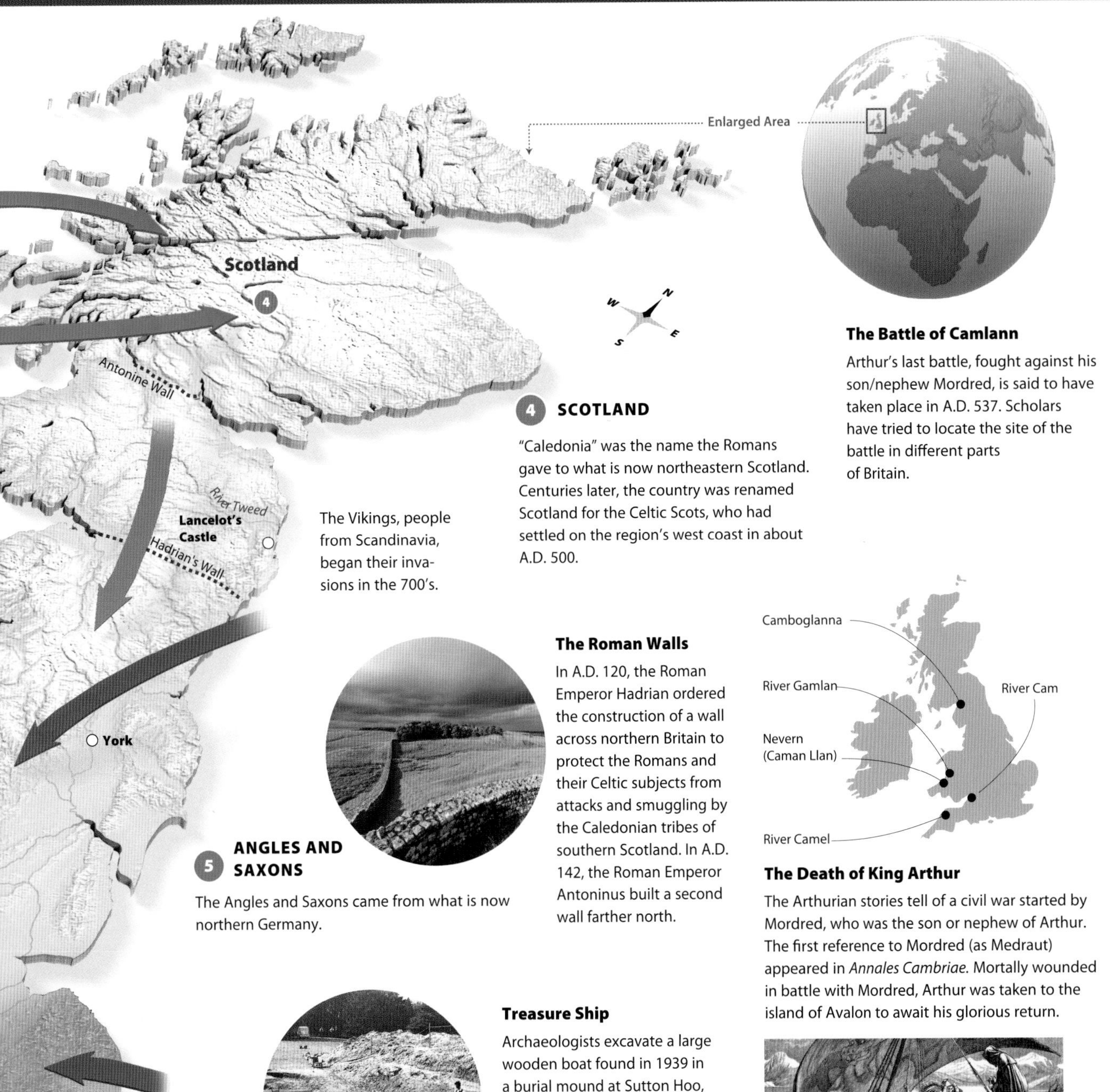

The Vikings, people from Scandinavia, began their invasions in the 700's.

4 SCOTLAND

"Caledonia" was the name the Romans gave to what is now northeastern Scotland. Centuries later, the country was renamed Scotland for the Celtic Scots, who had settled on the region's west coast in about A.D. 500.

The Battle of Camlann

Arthur's last battle, fought against his son/nephew Mordred, is said to have taken place in A.D. 537. Scholars have tried to locate the site of the battle in different parts of Britain.

The Roman Walls

In A.D. 120, the Roman Emperor Hadrian ordered the construction of a wall across northern Britain to protect the Romans and their Celtic subjects from attacks and smuggling by the Caledonian tribes of southern Scotland. In A.D. 142, the Roman Emperor Antoninus built a second wall farther north.

5 ANGLES AND SAXONS

The Angles and Saxons came from what is now northern Germany.

The Death of King Arthur

The Arthurian stories tell of a civil war started by Mordred, who was the son or nephew of Arthur. The first reference to Mordred (as Medraut) appeared in *Annales Cambriae*. Mortally wounded in battle with Mordred, Arthur was taken to the island of Avalon to await his glorious return.

Treasure Ship

Archaeologists excavate a large wooden boat found in 1939 in a burial mound at Sutton Hoo, near Suffolk, England. The boat, dating to about A.D. 650, contained the richest treasure ever unearthed in England.

The Jutes came from what are now northern Germany and Denmark.

The Faces of King Arthur

No one knows what Arthur looked like, if he even existed. Although he would have lived in the A.D. 500's, artists have traditionally dressed him in clothing from the Middle Ages, which ended in the 1400's.

Attributes of an Emperor

Arthur appears in an illustration from the mid-1200's displaying characteristics that clearly define his personality. Instead of being seated on a throne, the king sits on a collapsible military chair, in a reference to his role as a warrior and conqueror. The crowns that surround him symbolize the kings who submitted to him. His feet rest on an enemy's head. This illustration is from *Abbreviatio Chronicorum Angliae (Brief History of England),* written between 1250 and 1259 by Matthew Paris, a monk at St. Albans Abbey (now a cathedral).

WARRIOR
Sword raised, Arthur prepares to battle a foe in an illustration from the 1400's. He carries a shield with his standard coat of arms—three gold crowns on a blue background.

In Youth

Arthur is usually portrayed during one of two periods in his life—as a youth, just before or after becoming king, and as an old man, after long years on the throne. Youthful portraits often show him beardless and inexperienced. Images of Arthur in his youth include an illustration from the early 1300's (right) and a ceramic panel (far right) from the 1800's by English artist William Morris.

Death of the King

Arthur is comforted by Morgan le Fay (with book), his half-sister, in *The Death of King Arthur* (1887), an oil painting by Scottish artist James Archer. Arthur's death became a favorite theme of artists during the second half of the 1800's.

Coronation

Arthur is crowned king of the Britons, in images from two manuscripts from the Middle Ages.

Marriage

Arthur and Guenevere marry, in an illustration by John H. Bacon for a 1914 children's book with stories about the king and his knights.

In Old Age

Portraits of Arthur in his later years often show him as a venerable and respected figure, though inexpressive and inactive. Crowned and bearded, Arthur appears in a panel from a stained glass window at Bath Abbey (right) and a drawing by French artist Gustave Doré from the 1800's (far right).

Was Cadbury the Mythical Camelot?

Over the centuries, a number of sites have been identified as Camelot, the seat of King Arthur's court. The most popular is Cadbury Castle in Somerset.

Camelot is the center—and symbol—of the Legend of King Arthur. First named by Chrétien de Troyes in 1170, Camelot became Arthur's favorite dwelling and the starting point for the Quest for the Holy Grail. In modern times, Camelot has also come to represent a state of mind or a reflection of a lost ideal.

WHERE WAS CAMELOT?

A lack of evidence for a historical Arthur has not stopped authors from trying to locate his home. Geoffrey of Monmouth set Arthur's court at Caerleon Castle in Wales. According to Sir Thomas Malory, the castle was in Winchester. In the mid-1500's, a historian named John Leland linked Camelot with a hill fort at Cadbury in Somerset, based on an old tradition. The city of Glastonbury, associated with Arthur's tomb and the legendary Island of Avalon, are also in Somerset, just 15 miles (24 kilometers) away.

ARCHAEOLOGICAL CLUES

Cadbury Castle is not a castle but a hill fort that is 492 feet (150 meters) above sea level. Its summit is a small plateau. Hill forts were common natural defenses in prehistoric England and Ireland. They consisted of circular walls of earth reinforced by fences made of tree trunks or stones and protected by deep ditches.

Excavations in 1913 revealed that people had sought refuge from their enemies at the hill fort for thousands of years. The ancient Romans captured the site and established their own fort there.

In 1955, a local archaeologist exploring Cadbury found pieces of ceramic pottery that were similar to some found in Tintagel Castle in Cornwall, the legendary site of Arthur's birth. The fragments, which dated from the 500's and 600's, suggested that someone important had once lived in Cadbury Castle—someone wealthy enough to import luxury goods.

New excavations were conducted from 1966 to 1970 by the Camelot Research Committee, under the direction of Leslie Alcock. Their work confirmed that the Britons had fortified the hill on various occasions, building embankments, palisades, and towers. Alcock's excavations also unearthed the foundation of a wooden building that had been divided into at least two rooms. A larger room could have served as a throne room; a smaller room could have been a kitchen or a service area.

The Lake of the Lady

Dozmary Pool, about 10 miles (16 kilometers) from the sea in Cornwall, is linked by some traditions to the dwelling of Viviane, the Lady of the Lake. When the young Arthur, during battle, broke the sword he had pulled from the stone, Merlin the magician sent him to a lake. From the water there rose an arm holding a sword, while a beautiful maiden walked on the water. She was the Lady of the Lake, who lived in a castle under the waters. She gave the sword to Arthur, saying it would protect him so long as he wore its *scabbard* (case). This sword was the mythical Excalibur. After being mortally wounded by Mordred in Camlann, Arthur sent Sir Bedivere to return the sword to its guardian. When the knight threw the sword into the lake, a hand rose from the water and pulled it down.

CADBURY CASTLE

Cadbury, a hill fort in Somerset, England, is the most popular candidate for the home and headquarters of a historical King Arthur. It is widely known as Camelot in stories about the king.

Characters in the Legend

Colored by a patchwork of legends which took shape between the1100's and 1200's, the mythology of the Knights of the Round Table offers sometimes contradictory versions. Certain later works, such as *Le Morte d'Arthur* by Sir Thomas Malory, attempted to unify the stories.

The Characters of the Round Table

Although some specifics vary among the different Arthurian accounts, family ties of King Arthur and his main Knights of the Round Table can be traced throughout all of them.

Igraine

First appears in *Historia Regum Brittaniae* (1138). She becomes the wife of Uther Pendragon after her first marriage to Gorlois, Duke of Cornwall.

Uther Pendragon

The king of Britain and the father of Arthur. He seduces Igraine in the fortress of Tintagel after battling Gorlois at the Dimilioc Castle.

Morgause

Queen of Orkney, sister of King Arthur and wife of King Lot. In *Le Morte d'Arthur* (1485), she is the mother of the knights Gawain and Mordred.

Guenevere

Daughter of King Leodegrance of Cameliard. She becomes the wife of King Arthur. Her infidelity with Lancelot brings ruin to the Round Table.

Morgan le Fay

Sister of Arthur. In the early stories, she is charitable and takes care of Arthur in Avalon. In later stories, she opposes Arthur, but also bears his son Mordred.

Mordred

In some stories, Arthur's son, resulting from an incestuous relationship with Morgan le Fay. He is the traitor in the legend and corrupts the court of King Arthur and brings it to ruin.

Arthur

In his youth, he is recognized as a brilliant idealist and an undefeatable warrior. He is accepted as king thanks to Merlin the wizard. He repels the Anglo-Saxon invasions.

Merlin

Welsh wizard, central to the Arthurian legend and adviser to both Uther and Arthur. He ends his days in the forest of Brocéliande, under a spell cast on him by his companion Viviane.

The Lady of the Lake

Viviane, daughter of the king of Northumberland. She trains Lancelot and gives Arthur the sword Excalibur. In some accounts, she seduces Merlin and steals his secrets of magic.

Chronology of Major Arthurian Works

The main works that reference King Arthur are presented as historical treatises. The others are tales of chivalry.

830	1138	1155
Historia Brittonum	***Historia Regum Britanniae***	***Roman de Brut***
Nennius	Geoffrey of Monmouth	Wace
This chronicles the early history of England and Wales. It has the first mention of Arthur as a historical figure.	Pseudo-historical work based on *Historia Brittonum*, among other works. First mention of the sword Excalibur.	First mention of the Round Table.

Where is "Arthur's Burial Cross," which marked the site of his tomb at Glastonbury?

In 1191, the monks of Glastonbury Abbey discovered a tomb they identified as belonging to King Arthur. Along with his remains was found a cross which (whether or not a fraud) possesses undeniable historical value. The cross had an inscription in Latin: "Hic iacet sepultus inclitus rex Arturus in insula Avalonia" ("here lies buried the renowned King Arthur in the island of Avalon"). The cross disappeared in the 1700's and only a reproduction remains, which was made by historian William Camden in 1607.

The Legacy of Arthur

In 1485, Henry VII became the first Tudor king of England. He came from a noble Welsh family and used this origin to stake his claim to the throne as heir to Arthur. Before him, the Norman Plantagenet dynasty had used the Arthurian legend to gain the support of subjects of Celtic origin to fight against the Saxons, who were defeated by William of Normandy in 1066.

Galahad
The noblest knight of the Round Table. The son of Lancelot and Elaine, he is a descendant of Joseph of Arimathea.

Perceval
The main hero of the earliest stories regarding the Grail. Known as the "perfect fool."

Pellinore
King and loyal ally of King Arthur. He is the father of Percival. After he kills King Lot, the failure of his dynasty and of the Round Table begins.

Lionel
Brother of Sir Bors and cousin of Lancelot. He takes sides with Lancelot against King Arthur and is named King of Gaunes in Gaul.

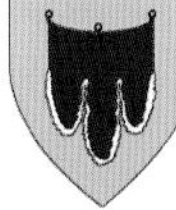

Bedivere
Marshal of Logres and companion of Arthur, he was born in Normandy and buried in Bayeux.

Kay
One of King Arthur's first knights. He is the steward of the kingdom and adopted brother of Arthur.

Lancelot
Son of King Ban of Benoic, he is adopted during infancy by the Lady of the Lake, who introduces him to Arthur. He embodies both the strength and weakness of the Round Table.

Gawain
The eldest son of King Lot of Orkney, he is a friend of Lancelot. In some versions of the story, he is mortally wounded by Lancelot after the death of Mordred.

Bors
The son of King Bohort, he is the brother of Lionel, and cousin of Lancelot. He is the only knight who after seeing the Grail returns to Camelot.

Tristan
A historical figure, he was the nephew of King Mark of Cornwall. His tomb, according to tradition, is near Fowey.

C. 1170
Lancelot, the Knight of the Cart
Chrétien de Troyes
First mention of Lancelot and Camelot, King Arthur's court. The poem was finished by Godefroi of Leigni.

1191
Perceval, the Story of the Grail
Chrétien de Troyes
Inspired by Celtic traditions and British legends, it mentions the Holy Grail for the first time.

C. 1200
Joseph of Arimathea, Merlin
Robert de Boron
These two works of French poetry clearly link the Holy Grail to Christianity.

C. 1210
Parzival
Wolfram von Eschenbach
Completes the unfinished work of Troyes, with new contributions regarding the origin of the Holy Grail.

1215/1235
The Vulgate Cycle
Anonymous
Five works that present the first unified structure of the legend. Galahad is introduced.

1485
Le Morte d'Arthur
Sir Thomas Malory
This brings together the various traditions of the Arthurian story. The most influential version in later times.

The Round Table

The brotherhood of the Knights of the Round Table has inspired artists for centuries. According to legend, Arthur decided to seat his knights around a circular table to avoid quarrels over who should occupy the seats of honor. Because the knights were all "noble and equal," no knight could boast of sitting higher than another.

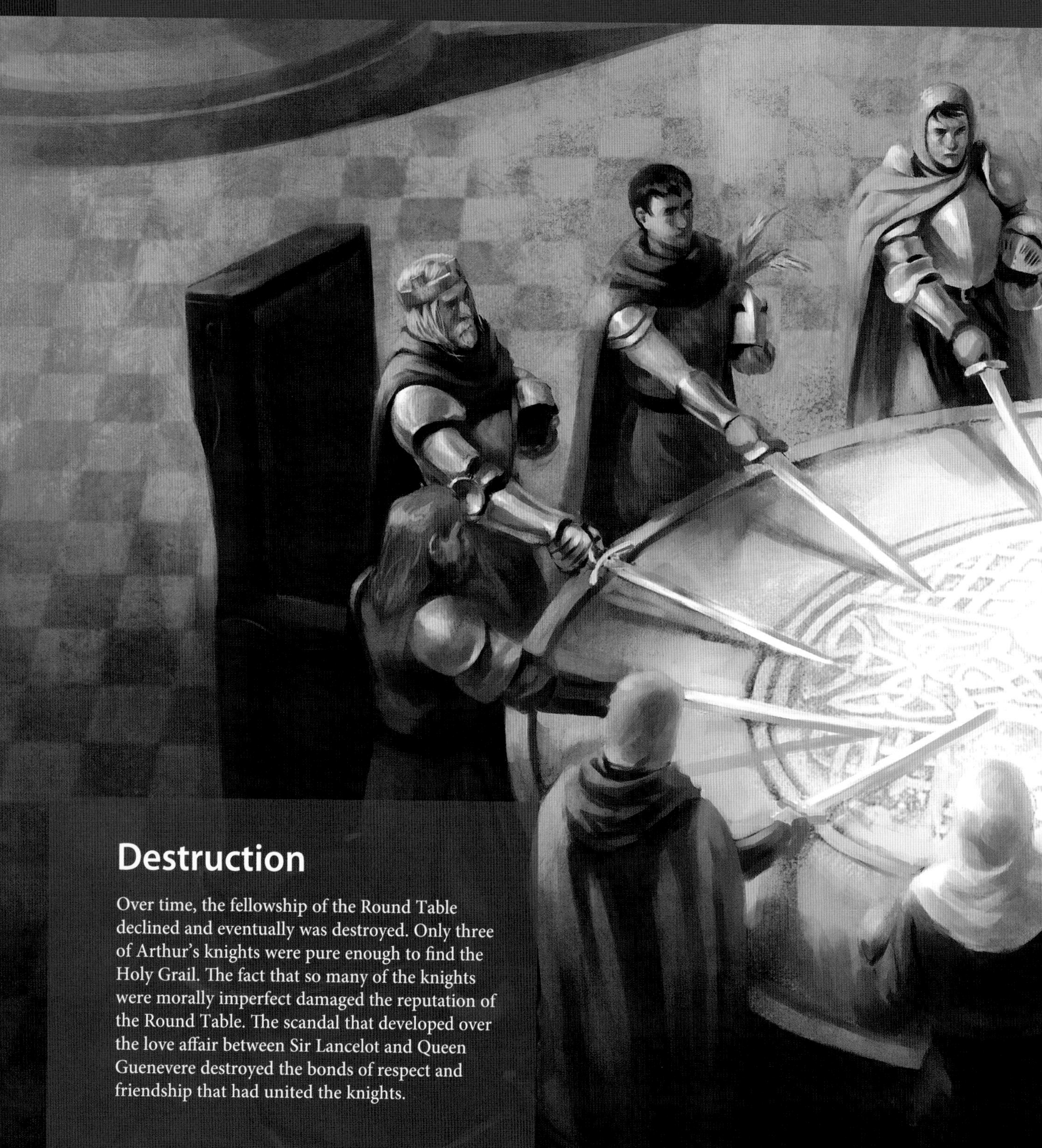

Destruction

Over time, the fellowship of the Round Table declined and eventually was destroyed. Only three of Arthur's knights were pure enough to find the Holy Grail. The fact that so many of the knights were morally imperfect damaged the reputation of the Round Table. The scandal that developed over the love affair between Sir Lancelot and Queen Guenevere destroyed the bonds of respect and friendship that had united the knights.

The Siege Perilous

Sir Galahad is presented to the Knights of the Round Table, in an illustration from the 1300's. Sir Galahad occupied the "Siege Perilous" (Perilous Seat), a chair reserved for a knight so pure that he would someday find the Holy Grail. Anyone who sat there without the right to do so would die in the act. Sir Galahad became one of three knights to find the Holy Grail.

MOVEABLE FEAST

In one version of the legend, the Round Table could seat 1,600 men, yet fold up so it could be carried on horseback.

NUMBER OF PLACES

The number of knights seated at the Round Table varies by author. Robert de Boron named 13 knights, an explicit reference to Jesus and the 12 Apostles.

Cruel Warrior or Righteous King?

The era in which the historical Arthur would have lived—the A.D. 500's—suffered from continuous wars and instability. There was little room for the chivalry of warriors.

The magnificent court of Camelot and the adventures of the Knights of the Round Table were idealizations of royal life that grew from the songs of minstrels in the 1000's and 1100's. In the 400's and 500's in Britain, warriors did not fight ferocious dragons. The real enemies were the Saxon, Angle, Jute, and Pict invaders.

THE PERFECT WARRIOR

The Arthur of legend was a king in shining armor who was surrounded by knights with perfect manners and flawless behavior. He and his knights lived in huge castles with halls dedicated to music and dance.

The "real" Arthur would have looked and lived quite differently. His best clothes would have included a linen jacket and leather vest, pants made of the same leather or linen, a woolen cloak that served as a cape to keep him warm in the winter, an iron and leather helmet, and leather boots. He would have carried a heavy iron sword.

Like his warriors, Arthur would have lived in a round house made of *wattle-and-daub* (a basketwork of thin branches [wattle] plastered with mud [daub] with a roof made of straw). Central fireplaces would have filled the house with smoke. The only furniture would have been a few low tables. People sat on the floor and slept on skins or mats.

THE CODE OF CHIVALRY

The legendary Arthur and his knights followed the code of chivalry, a version of royal life that developed as the first long narratives about Arthur began appearing. This code set standards for the behavior of all warriors—necessary because the life of a lord and his knights in the Middle Ages centered on fighting. The men of the ruling class believed that the only honorable way to live was as a warrior. When not making war, they practiced for war.

The minstrels portrayed true knights as men of faith who were ready to die for the church. They were loyal to their lords and used their strength to protect women and the feeble. They championed right against injustice and never surrendered in the face of the enemy.

Of course, in real life, knights did not always follow this high-minded code. The violent life of the Middle Ages made it difficult to prevent violations of the code. The honor and loyalty of the knights often applied only to members of their own ruling class. In addition, knights often acted brutally toward the common people, who had few rights. And even dedicated knights were interested in conquest and plunder.

The Mysterious Riothamus, King of the Britons

In A.D. 470, Sidonius Apollinaris, bishop of Clermont-Ferrand, wrote to a man named Riothamus, addressing him as the king of the Britons. Sidonius said that Riothamus was summoned by the Roman Emperor of the West, Anthemius, to assist in the campaigns against the Visigoths in what is now the Burgundy region of France. Riothamus crossed the English Channel with a 12,000-man army but was defeated after being betrayed by the governor of Burgundy. But his fame and reputation as a great king endured in Britain and could have inspired the later works of Chrétien de Troyes and other French authors.

IDEAL MONARCH

In English literature, Arthur is portrayed as a powerful king in both wartime and peacetime.

Who Was Merlin?

The character of Merlin is almost as important as that of Arthur in the legends of the English king. Magician, prophet, and political adviser, Merlin has even been credited with building Stonehenge.

Merlin appears in many of the stories about King Arthur. According to some narratives, he educated Arthur as a youth and advised him when he became the king. Merlin also helped to establish the Round Table. Merlin foresaw a number of important events, including the Quest for the Holy Grail and the destruction of Arthur's castle, Camelot. Merlin was also said to have transported to the Salisbury Plain the stone blocks used to build Stonehenge.

In some stories, Merlin plays a major role in Arthur's birth. King Uther Pendragon appealed to Merlin after he fell in love with Igraine, the wife of the Duke of Cornwall. With Merlin's help, Uther took the form of the duke and so conceived Arthur.

MERLIN'S DEBUT

The first writer to use the name "Merlin" in a story about King Arthur was Geoffrey of Monmouth. He established a large part of Merlin's character in *Prophetiae Merlini (The Prophecies of Merlin)* (1135) and other works. But the *idea* of Merlin is at least 200 years older than Geoffrey. A similar character called Myrddin appeared in a history of England and Wales written by the Welsh monk Nennius in the 800's and in the Welsh poems collected in the *Book of Taliesin* in the 900's.

These early accounts of Arthur describe Myrddin as a wizard and prophet, whose father was an evil spirit. Geoffrey's Merlin can talk to animals, including dragons, and control natural elements.

MERLIN THE BARD

The story of Merlin may have originated in legends of a Celtic bard who lived in the 500's. Bards were professional poets who sang about heroes, great deeds, and traditions. They generally accompanied themselves on a harp or other stringed instrument. That legendary bard may have been based on a man named Lailoken, who lived in Strathclyde (Scotland) and went mad when his king died in the Battle of Arfderydd.

MERLIN'S END

In later stories about King Arthur, Merlin makes the dreadful mistake of falling in love with Viviane, the ruler of the kingdom of Avalon. She is known as the Lady of the Lake. In some stories, she steals his magical secrets. In others, she refuses to return his love until he has taught her all he knows. She then uses her magic to imprison him forever in a tree trunk or under a rock.

KING'S TUTOR
Merlin the magician instructs a young Arthur, in an Italian manuscript from the mid-1300's.

Was Merlin a Druid?

Druids made up the learned, priestly class in Celtic society. Their main role was in overseeing religious activities and performing rituals. They practiced *divination* (predicting future events) by studying the flights of birds and the remains of sacrificed animals. They may have also sacrificed human beings. They venerated two sacred plants—the mistletoe and the oak.

Astrologers and healers, the Druids were also bards, who preserved the traditions of the community through their stories and songs. They advised tribal leaders on political matters, settled disputes, and made laws. The Romans tried to eliminate Druidism after they conquered Britain. By the 500's, Druidism had pretty much died out, as most Celts converted to Christianity.

What Was the Quest for the Holy Grail?

In stories written in the 1200's and afterward, Arthur was linked to one of the most important symbols of Christianity.

The search for the Holy Grail became the greatest of all of the adventures of the Knights of the Round Table. In early Celtic stories, the Grail was a mysterious food-producing vessel. It was usually depicted as a dish or cup. The Grail later became identified with the cup used by Jesus at the Last Supper. According to some stories, Joseph of Arimathea, a follower of Jesus, also used the cup to catch the blood of Jesus as he hung from the cross.

SEEKING THE GRAIL

According to Malory's *Le Morte d'Arthur* (1470), the search for the Grail began at a gathering of the knights at Arthur's castle. Suddenly, the Grail mysteriously appeared suspended in the air, filling the hall with brilliant light and sweet aromas. The vision inspired about 150 knights to search throughout Britain for the Grail.

The knights faced many dangers during their quest. Their actions revealed that only three of them—Bors, Galahad, and Perceval—were morally perfect and, therefore, fit to complete the quest.

FINDING THE GRAIL

After many years, the three knights entered Castle Corbenic, where Pelles was one of the rulers. There they saw a vision in which Joseph of Arimathea appeared as a priest. Angels brought in the Grail and the bloody spear that had pierced Jesus's side during the Crucifixion. A child appeared above the Grail and changed into bread. Then Christ emerged from the cup and gave Communion to the men. The vision was meant to prove that, in the Mass, the bread and wine are changed into the body and blood of Christ. Galahad used blood from the spear to heal Pelles, who had suffered a wound that would not heal.

The three knights then left the castle and sailed on a ship that, they discovered, carried the Grail. Guided by supernatural forces, the ship took the knights and the Grail to the distant city of Sarras. There, after Galahad died, Bors and Perceval saw the Grail rise into heaven. According to the legend, no one has seen the Holy Grail since that time.

THE GRAIL APPEARS
The Holy Grail appears to the Knights of the Round Table, in an illustration from a manuscript from the 1400's. Galahad occupies the place of honor.

Joseph of Arimathea

According to the Bible, Joseph of Arimathea was a wealthy Jew who lived at the time of Jesus. After the Crucifixion, Joseph received permission to take away the body of Jesus. He placed it in his own newly carved tomb.

A story written by Robert de Boron in about 1200 is the first to link Joseph to the Legend of King Arthur. For his tale, de Boron built on Chrétien de Troyes's *Perceval, or The Tale of the Grail,* the earliest known version of the legend of the Holy Grail.

According to de Boron, the Romans imprisoned Joseph because he was a follower of Jesus. Once Joseph was freed, he and a group of Christians carried the Grail throughout the Holy Land. Joseph later took the Grail to Britain, where he founded England's first Christian church, in Glastonbury. Joseph and his descendants then served as guardians of the Grail.

Glastonbury Tor

Glastonbury Tor is rich in history and legend. In the Legend of King Arthur, the tor was the Island of Avalon, the place where Arthur was taken after his last battle to recover from his wounds. In ancient times, the hill, known in Welsh as Ynys Afallach, may have been almost completely surrounded by a vast lake or marshland.

TERRACES

The seven terraces that surround the *tor* (hill) are one of the area's greatest mysteries. They are perfectly carved and may have been used for farming. However, some say that the terraces could be the remains of an ancient *labyrinth* (sacred pathway) created for religious purposes.

The Chalice Well

At the foot of the hill that rises to Glastonbury Tor, there is an ancient well, which is a crucial element of the mysterious mythology surrounding this place. Known as the Chalice Well, it is said to be the place where Joseph of Arimathea hid the Holy Grail.

2 SAINT MICHAEL'S TOWER
is the only surviving part of a church built in 1360 by Christian monks. The first church on the site was probably destroyed by a major earthquake that struck the area in 1275.

3 CONCRETE PATH
This walkway was constructed to offer a paved path to the summit, thus minimizing erosion caused by visitors taking a direct route to the top.

Glastonbury Abbey

For hundreds of years, people have journeyed to Glastonbury Abbey to see the site where, legend says, King Arthur was buried.

Glastonbury has been a center for Christian worship for more than 1,000 years. Joseph of Arimathea, who buried Jesus in his own tomb after the Crucifixion, figures in several stories about the establishment of the first church on the site. In one, Joseph built a *wattle-and-daub* (stick-and-mud) church here while visiting the British Isles in search of tin. In this legend, he was accompanied by the boy Jesus. In another story, Joseph founded a church here after fleeing the Holy Land with the Holy Grail after the Crucifixion.

According to historical and archaeological sources, the first *monastery* (community of monks) may have been established here in the A.D. 600's. Over the centuries, a number of churches have stood at the site. The monastery also grew in size and importance. By the 1100's, it was one of the wealthiest, most powerful abbeys in England. It also became the foremost center of learning in the country.

But disaster struck in 1184, when a huge fire destroyed the church and abbey. Aided by King Henry II, the monks began to rebuild. By 1186, they had completed the Lady Chapel, which still stands today. Three years later, they began work on a new church, which became known as the Great Church. Unfortunately, in that year, King Henry, Glastonbury's royal patron, died.

FINDING "KING ARTHUR"

Then in 1191, the monks announced a remarkable discovery—the tomb of King Arthur and Queen Guenevere. The chronicles relate that about 7 feet (2 meters) down, the monks found a lead cross. On it were inscribed the words "Hic iacet Sepultus inclitus Rex Arturius in insula Avalonia," Latin for "Here lies buried King Arthur in the island of Avalon."

Happily for the abbey's treasury, pilgrims began traveling from all over England to Glastonbury to see the tomb. In 1278, the remains were laid in caskets and moved to a marble tomb that was placed before the main altar in the abbey church.

LOST REMAINS

In the late1530's, however, Glastonbury Abbey, like other monasteries in England, was *dissolved* (shut down). After breaking with the Catholic Church in Rome, King Henry VIII began to seize the monasteries, taking for himself their vast land and great wealth.

Glastonbury Abbey also fell victim to the king. In 1539, the abbey and church were stripped of their valuable furnishings and art. The abbot was hanged on Glastonbury Tor. During the upheaval, the remains of Arthur and his queen disappeared.

Arthur at Glastonbury

The Legend of King Arthur is deeply intertwined with the history of Glastonbury. According to some stories, Arthur never died but sleeps at Glastonbury, waiting for a time when his country needs him again.

Royal Grave

King Henry II, an important financial supporter of Glastonbury Abbey, was convinced that King Arthur had been buried at the site and urged the monks to search for his tomb. According to an account written by a cleric named Gerald of Wales (1146-1223), Henry said he had learned from an aged bard that Arthur's body could be found on the abbey grounds. Henry said that Arthur had been buried 16 feet (5 meters) below the surface to prevent the king's Saxon enemies from finding him.

In 1191, two years after Henry's death, the monks of Glastonbury announced that they had finally found Arthur's grave. It lay, Gerald said, between two pyramids that had been erected long ago in Arthur's honor.

Gerald related how the monks discovered a skeleton of a man in an oaken coffin below a lead cross. The remains indicated that man was quite tall for his time and had numerous wounds on his huge skull. Only one of the wounds had not healed, the one that had apparently caused his death.

Next to the man's skeleton was the skeleton of a woman with a lock of hair that was "blonde and beautiful, twisted and braided with astonishing skill." One monk, hoping to claim the hair before any other, leaped into the grave. But when he touched the hair, it crumbled to dust.

FINDING ARTHUR

Workers uncover two skeletons that the monks at Glastonbury Abbey claimed were those of King Arthur and Queen Guenevere.

ARTHUR'S GRAVE

A plaque near the Lady Chapel at Glastonbury Abbey marks the site where the remains of King Arthur and Queen Guenevere were said to have been found.

JOSEPH OF ARIMATHEA
Joseph of Arimathea plants his staff on Wearyall Hill after arriving in England with the Holy Grail, in a stained glass window from the Church of St. Peter and St. Paul in Wiltshire, the United Kingdom.

The Glastonbury Thorn

The Glastonbury Thorn, also called the Sacred Thorn, is a hawthorn tree that flowers twice yearly, in winter and spring. Other kinds of hawthorn flower only once. According to tradition, the Sacred Thorn sprang from the ground where Joseph of Arimathea planted his staff at Wearyall Hill, at the base of Glastonbury Tor. Stories linking the Glastonbury Thorn and the legend of King Arthur first appeared in the 1200's.

Over the centuries, a series of trees have served as the Sacred Thorn. The average lifespan of this variety of hawthorn is about 100 years.

Some of the trees have met with violence. During the English Civil War (1642-1651), troops loyal to rebel leader Oliver Cromwell cut down and burned the tree because they considered the story of its origin a superstition. In 2010, a tree that had been growing at the site since 1952 was cut to a stump by vandals. The tree has since been replanted.

SACRED THORN
Symbol of a 2,000-year-old religious tradition, this Glastonbury Thorn tree stood on Wearyall Hill for more than 50 years before being vandalized in 2010.

Did King Arthur Exist?

Historical sources suggest that a number of kings and princes with this name lived between the 400's and 600's. However, the real identity of this character remains a mystery.

We may never know if the legend of King Arthur arose from the exploits of a real king. The first stories about Arthur were passed along by word of mouth. The bards who told these tales may have been singing of an actual British leader who won some battles against Germanic invaders in the early A.D. 500's. But the stories may just have been fantasies.

Nevertheless, over the centuries, historians have tried to identify King Arthur with various figures. Geoffrey of Monmouth stated that Arthur was the grandson of Constantine II, the Roman general who proclaimed himself Emperor of the West at the beginning of the 400's. Constantine left Britain defenseless as of 407, when he recalled his best men to Rome to fight in civil wars and against the continental barbarians. The departure of the Romans opened the door to Saxon invaders. According to Geoffrey, Arthur was, thus, a British king with Roman blood and noble origins.

ARTHURS EVERYWHERE

The name "Arthur" appears in several British regions. The Campbell *clan* (family) traces its roots to Arthur ic Uibar, a legendary warrior whose court was located by one scholar in Carlisle, Cumbria, an English county bordering Scotland. There is also a historical record of a King Arthwys, who lived approximately one generation before the traditional Arthur. His lands extended through the Northern Pennines, a mountain range considered the backbone of Great Britain.

ARTHURS IN WALES

Another possible source for Arthur is Prince Artuir, who lived in the mid-500's in Dumnonia. These lands bordering Cornwall produced some of the first Arthurian sagas.

The Welsh kingdom of Glywyssing and Gwent also had its King Arthur, Arthwys ap Meurig, who, according to historians, lived in the 600's. He had his court in Caerleon, the same city that Geoffrey of Monmouth and Wace associate with Arthur.

In Powys, another of the historic counties that made up Wales, there are two candidates. The first is Owain Ddantgwyn, a prince of the late 400's from the house of Cunedda. The second was his son, Cuneglasus, also known as Cynlas. One medieval writer states that Owain, nicknamed "the Bear" (Arth in Old Welsh), was defeated in battle by his nephew and buried near a pond. These elements of his story correspond with parts of the Arthurian legend, including Arthur's death after a battle against Mordred and his transfer to the Island of Avalon.

Finally, a King Arthur governed the small kingdom of Dyfed in Wales at the end of the 500's. The court of this king was referred to as Celliwig ("the forest") in

The Order of the Garter of Edward III

The influence of the Round Table concept—described first in 1155 in the writings of the Norman poet Robert Wace—caused a proliferation of recreational tournaments in the 1200's and 1300's. These galas and championships were considered similar to those held by the Knights of Camelot for the enjoyment of kings and the wealthy. In 1344, Edward III held one of these festivals in Windsor Castle. It lasted three days, and when it finished, the king promised to reconstruct the Round Table. Edward used the character of Arthur to bring glory to the Norman Plantagenet dynasty, to which he belonged. The legend also helped promote a feeling of national identity by appealing to a past linked to native British values. In 1348, he founded the Noble Order of the Garter. The order's emblem (below) is patterned on the emblem worn by the knights in the Windsor tournament. The order is now the oldest and most esteemed in the United Kingdom.

A GLORIOUS KING
Arthur is portrayed in a tapestry from the 1300's now owned by the Cloisters, a branch of the Metropolitan Museum of Art in New York City.

TINTAGEL CASTLE
Located on the west coast of Cornwall (southwestern England), this castle is, according to tradition, King Arthur's birthplace. Under the cliff, there is a cave where, according to the legend, the magician Merlin lived.

most of the traditional Welsh poems of the 1100's and 1200's. The *Trioedd Ynys Prydein (Welsh Triads)* describes Arthur as occupying one of the three tribal thrones of the British Isles. *Culhwch and Olwen* describes the first adventures of Arthur and his men.

ARTHUR IN CORNWALL

Along with Wales, the other notable Arthurian region is Cornwall. Here, there are no historical figures who can be linked to the legendary Arthur. As early as 1150, Arthur was described as "chief of the Cornwall battalions" in the poem "Ymddiddan Arthur a'r Eryr." And in 1113, even before the spread of *Historia Regum Brittaniae*, a chronicler stated that the local population might well pick a fight if someone doubted that King Arthur was still alive and was waiting for the right moment to return to his throne.

THE NAME IN QUESTION

Some scholars have suggested that "Arthur" was not actually a name. As in the case of Owain Ddantgwyn, it is possible that the name could actually be a nickname or a noble title.

Other sources argue that "Arthur" is actually a version of the Roman first name "Artorius." According to one theory, the name originated with Lucius Artorius Castus, a Roman commander who lived in the late 100's and early 200's. Artorius was a respected military leader based in what is now the city of York.

Some of Artorius's troops may also have been the inspiration for the Knights of the Round Table. In addition to Roman soldiers, Artorius commanded Sarmatian *mercenaries* (soldiers for hire). The Sarmatians were originally from the lands bordering the Black Sea, in what is now Ukraine. But advances by the Huns and Goths, as well as civil wars, led to the collapse of their kingdom. The Sarmatians were known for their bravery and discipline.

Lucius Artorius also captained a punitive expedition to Armorica, later called Brittany, in continental Europe. The memory of this could have become a part of popular folklore on both sides of the English Channel and served as an example for the Arthur of legend.

Ambrosius Aurelianus

Some people believe that King Arthur is no more than a literary impersonation of Ambrosius Aurelianus, a Celtic-Roman warrior who lived during the 400's. He was known to the Welsh as Emrys Wledig ("the Emperor") or Emrys Benaur ("Golden Head"). Although his origins are not clear, both Gildas and Bede state that he led the British-Celtic troops in the battle of Mount Badon (pictured above), which was a great victory over the Saxons. Much later, Nennius and Geoffrey of Monmouth eulogized this person. Geoffrey states that Ambrosius and his father, Uther, escaped the persecution of Vortigern, who had seized the throne, and took refuge in Brittany. After recruiting a strong army, they returned to reclaim Uther's throne. Ambrosius and Uther were assisted by Merlin the magician in recovering the crown, which Ambrosius wore with justice and nobility until his death.

Stonehenge

According to Geoffrey of Monmouth, the magician Merlin used his powers to move the enormous stone circle (originally constructed by giants, said Monmouth) from Ireland to England. He did it to comply with the wishes of King Ambrosio Aureliano, who wanted to erect a monument in honor of dead British warriors. According to the legend, Uther Pendragon, Arthur's father, was buried there.

Traces of a Legend

For centuries, historians and others have tried to identify specific objects with King Arthur. An inability to prove that Arthur ever really existed has complicated the effort. But Celtic objects from the 400's and 500's can shed light on a time when Arthur could have lived.

Round Table

This replica of the Round Table has hung in the Great Hall of Winchester Castle in England for more than 700 years. The table was probably made in about 1290 to celebrate the betrothal (engagement) of a daughter of King Edward I. The table, which is made of English oak, measures 18 feet (5.5 meters) in diameter and weighs 2,650 pounds (1,200 kilograms). Originally, the table was not painted. King Henry VIII ordered it painted for a visit to England by King Charles V of France in 1522.

The table is divided into 24 places, with the names of the legendary Knights of the Round Table written around the edge. A special seat at the top displays a representation of King Arthur—with Henry VIII's features. The Tudor Rose—an emblem of the house of Henry VIII—dominates the center of the table.

SACRED HEAD

To the Celts, the head was the center of spiritual power. Its importance is seen in such Arthurian stories as "Sir Gawain and the Green Knight," which involves a "beheading game."

ROMAN SWORD

The sword carried by a real King Arthur probably resembled a Roman spatha. The iron sword was usually about 36 inches (90 centimeters) long. The upper photo shows the sword covered in rust, before it was restored.

The Welsh Flag

The dragon on the flag of Wales has been a Welsh symbol for nearly 2,000 years. The flag, officially adopted in 1959, features a red dragon on two horizontal stripes. According to tradition, the red dragon was the symbol of Arthur and his father, Uther Pendragon. The flag was flown by Henry Tudor in 1485 during the battle in which he defeated Richard III and captured the English throne. As king, Henry VII used the dragon to represent the newly established House of Tudor. Henry, who was fond of the Arthurian tales, named his first son Arthur.

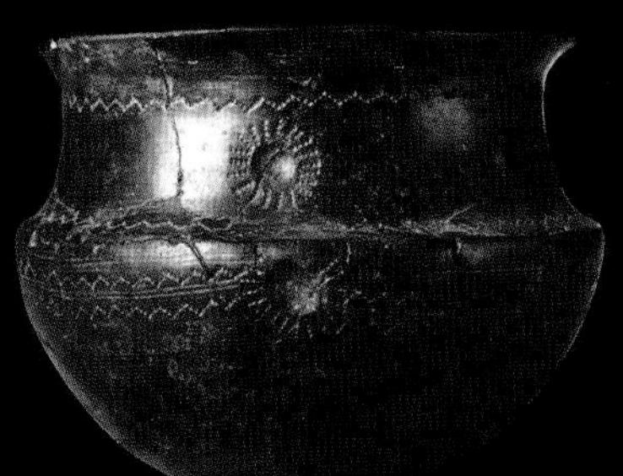

CAULDRON
Cauldrons were an important part of daily life for the Celts. The vessels were also widely used for religious rituals.

Chalice of Antioch

In the 1920's, several scholars argued that this highly ornamented silver cup, known as the Chalice of Antioch, was the Holy Grail, the cup used by Jesus at the Last Supper. The search for the Grail is a major theme in the Arthurian legend. The cup, which is 7 1/2 inches (19 centimeters) tall, was discovered in about 1910, probably in Turkey. Studies have determined that the cup dates from the early 500's. Some scholars have suggested that the "chalice" may have actually been used as a floor lamp in a church.

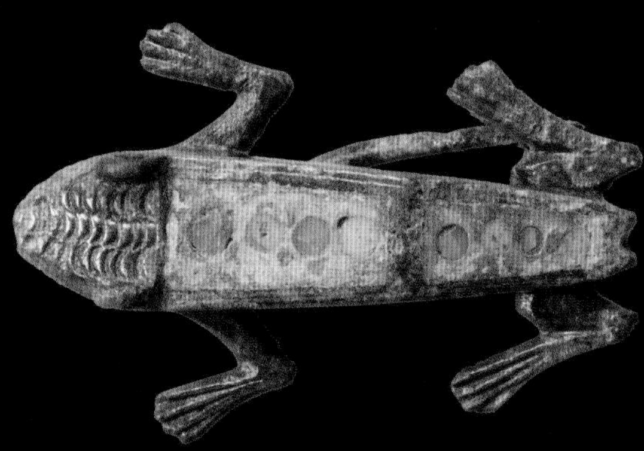

CELTIC ORNAMENTS
Ornamental objects called fibulas, such as this bronze frog with enamelwork from the 300's, were commonly used by the Celts to fasten their clothing. Fibulas were also worn as *talismen* (objects supposed to have magic powers).

ANCIENT CROSS
The cross of St. Piran (patron of Wales, who lived in the 300's) measures 8 feet (2.4 meters) tall and is one of the oldest Celtic crosses in Cornwall. The circle at the top (a symbol of life for the Celts) is larger than in later versions of the Celtic cross.

Places to See and Visit

OTHER PLACES OF INTEREST

TINTAGEL CASTLE
CORNWALL, ENGLAND

According to tradition, this was Arthur's birthplace. In reality, the castle dates from the 1200's, though there are signs of occupation dating to the time of the Romans. Later retellings place King Mark of Cornwall, Tristan's uncle, in the castle. In 1998, "Arthur's Stone" was found here.

CADBURY CASTLE
SOMERSET, ENGLAND

Not a true castle but a hill fort, which shows evidence of having been inhabited since the Neolithic Period. The remains of a fortress constructed during the first centuries of the Christian era stand out. This is one of the primary candidates for the location of Camelot.

DOZMARY POOL
CORNWALL, ENGLAND

A small lake identified as the home of the Lady of the Lake, who delivered Excalibur to King Arthur at that same lake. The sword was returned upon King Arthur's death by Sir Bedivere, who threw it into the lake, where a hand (that of the Lady of the Lake) rose from the water and caught it.

ST. MICHAEL'S MOUNT
CORNWALL, ENGLAND

A tidal island off Cornwall's western coast washed by the English Channel to the south and the Celtic Sea to the north and west. According to the poet Lord Tennyson in *Idylls of the King,* this was the location of the final battle between King Arthur and Mordred. It is also believed that this battle took place in the Isles of Scilly.

WINCHESTER CASTLE
HAMPSHIRE, ENGLAND

Within the castle, which was built in the mid-1000's, only the great hall

The Seats of the Court

GLASTONBURY
A commercial center in Celtic times, Glastonbury is the location most often linked to Arthurian legend. Glastonbury Tor (left), the highest hill in the area, has been identified with the legendary Avalon. It is said that Joseph of Arimathea arrived in Glastonbury from the Holy Land, carrying the Grail. In 1191, the monks at Glastonbury Abbey said that they had found the tomb of Arthur and Guenevere.

STIRLING CASTLE
Some researchers maintain that both King Arthur and Merlin the magician were Scottish and place the king's mythical Round Table in Stirling Castle (far left). Outside of the legend, this complex is in fact one of the largest and best-preserved in Scotland and played a defensive role in the country's war for independence in the 1300's.

CAERLEON
Located in southern Wales, near the English border, this castle was named as the location of Arthur's court before it was moved to Camelot, in early versions of the Arthurian legend. Ruins of a Roman fortress (Isca Augusta) have been uncovered here, and it is thought that the amphitheater may have inspired the story of the Round Table.

Arthur's Great Hall

Opened to the public in the 1930's, King Arthur's Great Hall was built in the city of Tintagel, Cornwall. It is the only building in the world entirely dedicated to King Arthur. Housing a great artistic heritage with an outstanding specialized art gallery, the Round Table, thrones, weapons, and other pieces from the period have been re-created here. In addition, 72 stained glass windows recount the legend of the king and show the coats of arms belonging to his knights.

has survived. A replica of the Round Table, constructed around 1290 during the reign of Edward I, is kept there. Sir Thomas Malory identified Winchester with Camelot.

CASTELL DINAS BRAN
WALES
The current building, on a hill near Llangollen, is from the 1200's, but there have been fortifications here since the A.D. 600's. The castle was a source of inspiration for the Grail's place of residence. Malory calls the castle where the Grail resided "Corbenic" (raven in old French).

CARMARTHEN
WALES
Region in South Wales where, according to tradition, Merlin was born. It is said that Merlin was trapped in a nearby cave, Bryn Myrddin ("Merlin's Hill"), after being cursed by the fairy Viviane. Carmarthen is one of the two locations in Wales where there are Roman amphitheaters (the other is Isca Augusta).

Glossary

Abbey—A building or buildings where monks or nuns live a religious life, ruled by an abbot or abbess; also known as a monastery.

Angles—One of the Germanic peoples who invaded Britain during the A.D. 400's and 500's. They came from Angeln, a district in what is now Schleswig-Holstein, and from the southern part of the Danish peninsula. The name *England* came from an Anglo-Saxon word that meant *Angle folk* or *land of the Angles.*

Archaeologist—A scientist who studies the remains of past human cultures.

Bards—Ancient singer-poets who sang about the heroes, accomplishments, and customs of a nation, generally accompanying themselves on a harp or other stringed instrument.

British Isles—A major group of islands, including Great Britain (made up of England, Scotland, and Wales), Ireland, the Isle of Man, the Hebrides, the Orkney Islands, the Shetland Islands, and about 5,500 small islands and islets.

Brittany—A region in northwestern France that was settled during the A.D. 400's to 600's by Celts from what are now the United Kingdom and Ireland. *Brittany* means *Little Britain.*

Camelot—King Arthur's favorite dwelling and the starting point of the Quest for the Holy Grail.

Celts—A diverse group of ancient inhabitants of Europe connected by a shared language, religion, and material culture. The term has also traditionally included the people of Iron Age Great Britain and Ireland.

Code of chivalry—Standards for the behavior of fighting men.

Culture—A term used by social scientists for a way of life. Culture includes a society's arts, beliefs, customs, institutions, inventions, language, technology, and values. A culture produces similar behavior and thought among most people in a particular society.

Divination—The practice of trying to learn about the un-known by magical or supernatural means.

Druids—Celts who oversaw religious activities and performed rituals for their tribe. They also practiced divination and acted as advisers to Celtic leaders.

Hill fort—A common natural defense in ancient Britain and Ireland consisting of the summit of a hill fortified with circular walls of earth reinforced by fences made of tree trunks or stones and deep ditches.

Holy Grail—Originally a mysterious food-producing vessel that later became identified with the cup used by Jesus at the Last Supper.

Iron Age—A period when the use of iron became widespread, beginning in about 1200 B.C.

Jutes—A Germanic tribe that invaded England between about A.D. 450 and the late 500's. The Jutes are thought to have come from what is now Denmark and northern Germany. They settled in parts of southeastern Britain that are now known as Kent, southern Hampshire, and the Isle of Wight.

Legend—A type of folk narrative that is set in the present or in the historical past. Although legends may have religious implications, most are not religious in nature. Legends distort the truth, but they are usually based on real people or events.

Minstrels—Professional entertainers who flourished in Europe during the Middle Ages. They were chiefly singers and musicians, but many were also storytellers, jugglers, clowns, and tumblers.

Myth—A story told to explain the world and its mysteries.

Picts—A people of ancient and medieval Scotland.

Ritual—A solemn or important act or ceremony, often religious is nature.

Quest—An important search for someone or something.

Round Table—A circular table at which King Arthur sat with his knights. It was circular to prevent the knights from quarreling over the place of honor.

Saxons—A Germanic people who invaded Britain during the 400's and 500's and settled in southern and eastern Britain. They were the greatest enemy of King Arthur and the Celts.

Scots—A Celtic tribe from northern Ireland that settled on Scotland's west coast in about A.D. 500.

Society—People living together as a group.

Tintagel—A castle on the west coast of Cornwall that is the traditional birthplace of King Arthur.

Tor—A high, rocky, or craggy hill.

Wattle-and-daub—A building material consisting of a basketwork of thin branches plastered with mud that was used to make houses.

For Further Information

Books

Harkins, Susan Sales., and William H. Harkins. *The Life and Times of King Arthur: The Evolution of a Legend.* Hockessin, DE: Mitchell Lane, 2007. Print.

Lee, Tony, and Sam Hart. *Excalibur: The Legend of King Arthur, a Graphic Novel.* Somerville, MA: Candlewick, 2011. Print.

Mersey, Daniel, and Alan Lathwell. *King Arthur.* Long Island City, NY: Osprey Pub., 2013. Print.

Mullarkey, Lisa, Howard McWilliam, and Howard Pyle. *Howard Pyle's King Arthur and the Knights of the Round Table.* Edina, MN: Magic Wagon, 2010. Print.

Snyder, Christopher A. *The World of King Arthur.* New York: Thames & Hudson, 2011. Print.

Websites

The Camelot Project: A Robbins Library Digital Project. University of Rochester, n.d. Web. 02 Feb. 2014.

"Guinevere's Wedding." *Wales History*. BBC, 2014. Web. 03 Feb. 2014.

"King Arthur." *Wales History.* BBC, 2014. Web. 03 Feb. 2014.

"King Arthur's Round Table Revealed." *History.* AETN UK, 2014. Web. 03 Feb. 2014.

"The Quest for the Holy Grail." *British Library.* The British Library Board, n.d. Web. 03 Feb. 2014.

Index

R

S

T

U

V

W

Acknowledgments

Pictures:

© AGE Fotostock
© Alamy Images
© Richard Barber
© Corbis Images
© Judith Dobie, English Heritage Graphics Team
© Getty Images
© Granger
© Other Images
© Philip Rahatz, Columbia University Archives
© Science Photo Library
© Topfoto
© University of Glasgow Archive Services, ref. GB0248 UP1/553/1